Dad's Girl

by

Kathy Coatney

Dad's Girl

Copyright @ 2015 by Kathy Coatney

www.kathycoatney.com

All rights reserved. No part of this publication can be reproduced, stored in a retrieval system, or transmitted in any form or by any means, electonic, mechanical, photocopying, recording or otherwise, without the prior permission of the copyright owner.

Windtree Press
4660 NE Belknap Court, Suite 101-0
Hillsboro, OR 97124
http://windtreepress.com

CONTENTS

Dedication . . . . Pg iv

Acknowledgements . . . . Pg v

Dad's Girl. . . . . Pg 1

Author Biography . . . . Pg 30

Dedication

To all the children who've lost a parent.

Acknowledgements

I've had a number of life-altering moments in my life, each special in their own way. The road to becoming a children's author has been smooth and rocky, but it has been an incredible journey because of those who have accompanied me. On this journey, I've also had the pleasure to work with several talented businesswomen: Susan Crosby, my editor, Yvonne Betancourt, my formatter and Tara, my cover designer.

This particular book moved me deeply as it's a true story, and the husband, father, son, nephew and friend we lost is missed every day.

A special thanks to Lily and her mom for sharing this story of the special man they called husband and Dad.

Dad's Girl

My name is Lily and I'm six-years-old.

My dad was the best dad ever.

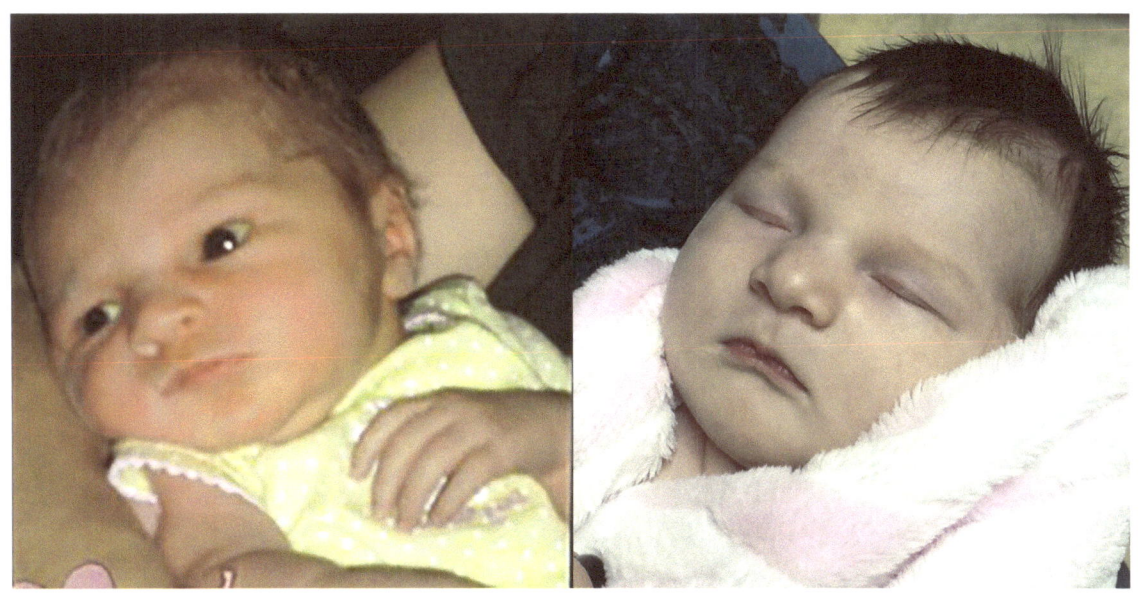

Lily	Violet

My dad died before my sister, Violet, was born, so I'm telling this story so she will know all the special things about him.

I look like my dad. I have his hair, eyelashes, eyeballs, nose, and I'm extroverted (that means I like to talk or so mom says).

Before I was even born he would talk to me through mom's belly (maybe that's why I'm extroverted).

Dad always took good care of me and mom by making sure we were safe and happy.

There were lots of things I loved about him.

His laugh, and playing with him. He used to tickle me and make me laugh.

Sometimes he would jump out at me and yell "Boo!" He'd scare me and I'd scream, then laugh.

Dad loved to BBQ, and he made my favorite food, steak. (Dad was <u>not</u> a vegetarian.)

I loved his famous macaroni and cheese made with white sauce, too.

Some of my favorites memories are the trips me, Mom and Dad took.

When I was little, we took our boat out to the lake and he would let me steer it.

Me and Uncle James in Disneyland

We went to Disneyland, too, and he and Uncle James took me on the Matterhorn and Thunder Mountain.

They were my favorite rides because they went really fast.

We went to Siskiyou and Donner Lakes and sometimes we rented a cabin with our friends at Donner Lake.

We went swimming in the lake, and the water was soooo cold I curled around Dad's neck to get warm.

We have an olive orchard that Dad loved to work in.

We would all go to the orchard—me, mom, and Mia, our black lab. Dad always sang about Mia, "Here she comes to wreck the day!" and we would all laugh.

I used to ride on the tractor with Dad, while he pushed the brush to the burn pile.

Fridays were Dad's day off, and we did special things together while mom taught school. We called it Dad and Lily day.

On Friday's before I started kindergarten, we would play together, then take a rest before going to Burger King for lunch. I always ordered nuggets and fries.

After I started kindergarten, Dad would take me to get a chocolate donut (my favorite!), then drive me to school.

He would stay and be classroom dad on Friday's. He made me laugh when Mackenna, a girl in my class came over and he said, "Mackenna, oh, there ya are."

My dad was always funny and made me laugh.

    I wish I could talk to Dad again and tell him about all the things that are happening, like Violet being born the day before Halloween, and all the hair she has, and how she looks just like him!

The one thing I wish more than anything is that I could hug him and tell him I love him again.

Mom, me and Violet

Author Biography

California native Kathy Coatney has spent long hours behind the lens of a camera wading through rice paddies, dairies and orchards during her twenty-year career as a photojournalist specializing in agriculture. She has most recently taken on the role of editor for West Coast Nut magazine.

She and her husband grow table olives and her family roots in agriculture run four generations deep, so Kathy knows farming from the ground up. Concerned that kids today don't have the exposure to farms and rural life that teaches them how their food is produced, she envisioned a new direction for her writing and launched *From the Farm to the Table*, a series of non-fiction children's books about agriculture.

Kathy's always been a believer in jumping into the deep end of the pool and learning to swim later, whether it's venturing into self-publishing, mountain biking or cross-country skiing.

Happily married for over thirty-five years, she and her husband have two grown sons, a new granddaughter and a menagerie of animals—a black lab who thinks she's human, a house cat that looks part bobcat, and half a dozen cottontails that roam freely on her property.

Kathy also loves—and writes—deeply emotional, feel-good contemporary romances under the pen name Kate Curran.

View her photos at: Design Pics (www.agstockimages.com)
Like her at: www.facebook.com/katecurranauthor
Follow her on twitter @Katecurran3Kate
Visit her website at: www.kathycoatney.com

www.ingramcontent.com/pod-product-compliance
Lightning Source LLC
Chambersburg PA
CBHW050757110526
44588CB00002B/35